Beatrice M. A. Ash
with Lucile Allen

A TIME TO LIVE, A TIME TO DIE

Important Concerns When Death Draws Near

Augsburg

MINNEAPOLIS

A TIME TO LIVE, A TIME TO DIE
Important Concerns When Death Draws Near

Scripture quotations unless otherwise noted are from the New Revised Standard Version of the Bible, copyright © 1989, Division of Christian Education of the National Council of the Churches of Christ in the United States of America.

Cover design: Lecy Design
Interior design: Karen Buck

Library of Congress Cataloging-in-Publication Data

Ash, Beatrice M.A., 1932-
    A time to live, a time to die : important concerns when death
draws near / Beatrice M.A. Ash with Lucile Allen.
        p.   cm.
    ISBN 0-8066-2664-X (alk. paper):
    1. Death—Religious aspects—Christianity.   2. Terminally ill—
Religious life.   3. Spiritual life—Christianity.   4. Large type
books.   I. Allen, Lucile.   II. Title.
BT825.A75   1993
248.8'6—dc20   93-24243
                                                                              CIP

The paper used in this publication meets the minimum requirements of American National Standard for Information Sciences—Permanence of Paper for Printed Library Materials, ANSI Z329.48-1984. ∞™

Manufactured in the U.S.A.   AF 9-2664

97   96   95   94   93   1   2   3   4   5   6   7   8   9   10

To the memory of Jim Shipley—red-haired, freckle-faced, and fun-loving—who at eighteen, did his level best to make the world a better place for those around him. As Jim neared death, he insisted that I learn to care for the dying as well as the living so that I could be a better minister. What measure of success I have achieved is due initially to Jim.

CONTENTS

PREFACE

This book is about one of life's greatest mysteries—one that most people are curious about, everyone will experience, but about which few like to think or talk. It's about dying. More specifically, it's about the peace and joy that come with being prepared to "die well."

We all know we're going to die sometime, but if you are reading this book, chances are that you have reason to believe that your death may be imminent. Perhaps your doctor has just given you the news that you have a terminal illness, or the disease that you hoped would be cured by now has taken a turn for the worse. Or possibly you are approaching the natural end of a long, full life.

Whatever the reason, if you are facing the possibility of death, then you are probably feeling a wide range of emotions—fear, anger, perhaps even relief. I have written this book to let you know that it's okay to run the whole gamut of feelings, and to give you some guidance along the way. I will try to help you move through the sometimes overwhelming emotions toward practical, productive choices that can benefit you—and, perhaps even more so—the loved ones you may be leaving behind.

The way that a person handles death is colored by every experience he or she has had in life. There are no "right" answers to the questions, "How am I supposed to feel?" or "How am I supposed to act?" Everyone will act and react uniquely.

I have confronted my own death through a life-threatening accident and three potentially fatal illnesses. As a minister and hospice caregiver, I have also held the hands of more than a hundred dying persons and their families.

Out of these experiences I have identified seven concerns that, if taken seriously and acted upon, seem to make the difference between dying in a state of denial or dying after having achieved peace with God and others. These concerns touch on the physical, material, emotional, and spiritual elements of facing death, and each is covered in one chapter of this book.

None of the seven concerns is carved in stone. Quite the opposite—each one can overlap with the others, and some may not apply to your particular situation at all.

I do not expect (or even advise) you to address these concerns on your own. Many of my suggestions call for the cooperation and assistance of others.

I suggest that you read through all the chapters and then read them again, allowing different things to speak to you each time. My earnest prayer is that you allow God to walk through these pages with you—for God is the one who can truly help us prepare to "die well."

ACKNOWLEDGMENTS

I would like to acknowledge, with gratitude:

all those who trusted me enough to allow me into their sacred space as they dealt with impending death;

the nurses of the Hospice of Windsor, for their dedication to bringing wholeness to those they serve (these beautiful ladies exemplify what it means to be a nurse, and I am grateful to them for working with me to bring a measure of spiritual health to those under the care of Hospice);

my editor, Lucy Allen, who took my written words, my thoughts, and my intentions, and made them come together in a coherent manner;

Betty Rutherford—librarian, reader, coach, and friend—and Madeline Crnec, chiropractor, who massaged the aches as I wrote and helped so much with making sense when I got carried away with rhetoric;

Mary McCormick, secretary *extraordinaire*, who read lines between lines between lines—and can still smile;

Virginia Lauzon, my friend, who laughed and cried with me and made sure that I went out to play; and

ACKNOWLEDGMENTS

Dr. Dorothy Ley and Dr. John Morgan of Kings College, London, Ontario, for their encouragement and assistance.

I am also indebted to many others whose concepts and teachings I have used until they have become part of me and the way I minister. I have tried to give them due credit, and I apologize for any unintentional omissions.

one

HAVING OTHERS PRESENT

The experience of dying is most likely not something that you asked for or now look forward to going through. It's the last thing you wanted. Yet you still have to take responsibility for the process of preparing to die.

The valley of death is full of ironies. Perhaps you are wishing that people would just go away and leave you to die in peace—but feel hurt and angry when they do.

Just at the time when you feel uncertain, full of turmoil, and least capable of making logical decisions, you have to make the hardest ones of your life.

The greatest paradox of all is that death is life's ultimate solitary experience, yet no one should die alone. I witnessed the tragic results when one woman tried.

Linda, the forty-one-year-old mother of two sons, ages seventeen and twelve, was divorced from her husband, the father of her first son. She had lived for a brief time with the father of her second son, but they had separated and she had lost all contact with him. Linda struggled to provide for the boys on her hairdresser's income, making sure that no one knew of her truly desperate financial situation.

One day Linda discovered a lump in her breast. She ignored it for several months, but finally had surgery. The lump was malignant. She should have begun chemotherapy immediately. Instead, she ignored the doctor's advice and swore him to secrecy about her condition.

As time went on, Linda's brother and two of her aunts grew increasingly concerned about her health. She was having difficulty breathing, and her motor skills were deteriorating. Time after time, Linda refused to talk to anyone about her illness or to see a doctor.

One of her aunts went to Linda's doctor, but he, also, refused to divulge any details. He did say, however, that if Linda had not been treated in the last seven years, her condition must indeed be serious. He could give no further information without Linda's permission.

Linda's secret was discovered when she fell and broke her hip. She was taken to the hospital, where doctors diagnosed cancer that had metastasized. Now all over Linda's body, the cancer was in its final stages. She had just weeks to live.

Eventually, members of the family gathered at Linda's bedside, where an oxygen mask and other life-support systems kept her alive. She was conscious and aware of the people around her, but unable to speak.

Having been called in by the family, I approached Linda's bed. The strong smell of cigarette smoke was evident, even though she hadn't smoked for three days.

The hospice nurse introduced me. In reaction to my clerical collar, Linda began frantically shaking her head. A look of panic filled her face like that of a child threatened with severe punishment. I tried to comfort and reassure her, but the panic only increased. Finally I moved away.

Later, in the waiting room, Linda's aunt said, "She's dying the way she lived—the hard way. When her husband left she didn't tell anyone that she had no money and no food." Shaking her head, she added sadly, "What is family for, anyway?"

I asked her, "Had you known she was sick, what could you have done for her?"

"Nothing," she said, "absolutely nothing. She never let anyone do anything for her. That's why her husband and her boyfriend left."

Linda died three days later, still panic-stricken.

The Agony of Silence

Linda's refusal to share the news of her terminal illness with her family had a number of severe consequences. First, it gave fear control over her life. It's possible that fear killed Linda, not cancer, because it prevented her from getting treatment. Even after the cancer had spread, she could have spent her final few months helping her children grieve and prepare for life without her. Instead, in her denial, she made little provision for the care of her hurt and grief-stricken children. Her brother had promised to take care of the boys, but that was something his wife had not agreed to or looked forward to, since they had three young children of their own.

Linda's oldest son was furious that his mother hadn't trusted her family, and that she had valued her own life so little. He felt that his mother's death was totally unnecessary. Even worse, he was convinced that she refused treatment because she didn't love them.

It took many months for the family to work through their anger with Linda and her doctor for allowing her condition to deteriorate so drastically without the family's knowledge. No one benefited from Linda's silence, and many people were deeply wounded by it.

Your Valley of Death

This is a time when, more than ever, you need to be open and honest with the people closest to you. You need to be with people who love you—who can weather the ups and downs in your valley of death, who won't be offended by your deepest, darkest thoughts or feelings, and who can share the joy of all your victories.

You could, like Linda, try to keep your impending death a secret. You might think, *Who needs to know, anyway? I don't want people's pity. It would be awkward, because they don't know what to say to me and I don't know what to say to them.* You're right. You will probably experience every awkward reaction imaginable in yourself and others. But those are things you can live with and work through. What you don't want to do is to cause unnecessary agony for yourself and your loved ones by trying to face death alone.

Find a Friend

It isn't necessary to tell your deepest feelings to everyone, but there should be someone you can be completely honest with, and to just be with—someone who can provide comfort and a sense of security. That person could be your spouse, another family member, a longtime friend, or a clergyperson you can trust. More than anything, this person needs to be able to listen to your feelings—without censure—if you need to cry, or swear, or pray. And it needs to be someone to whom you can freely say, "I need to be alone."

You will be taking a risk by making your need known. What if the people you need most can't handle the thought of your death? What if they can't be around you because they are trying to deal with their own pain? What if they reject you when you need them most?

When Jesus faced death he admitted that he needed his disciples. His closest friends repeatedly disappointed him, but that didn't stop him from asking them to share his darkest hour. It is well worth the effort to find the right person to be there for you.

Life Goes On

After establishing such a key relationship, your immediate family should be informed if your death is imminent. You need their help, and they need yours, to cope with the drastic changes going on.

Mundane concerns such as "What's for dinner?" "Does the lawn need mowing?" or "Do the children have clean school clothes?" can seem like an insult to the way you're feeling at the moment. Yet an hour later you may be intensely interested in the details of life outside your room. Nothing fits together at a time like this, and it probably won't for a while, but you can help each other maintain a sense of balance and normalcy.

If your illness has been extensive, your loved ones need sufficient rest to carry on. Things still have to be done to run a household, such as cooking, cleaning, laundry, and grocery shopping. Relatives and friends could relieve stress for the whole family by helping in those areas. If you normally do things such as handle the correspondence or pay the bills, you can continue to do them from your hospital bed as long as your strength allows.

It is especially important that life continue as normally as possible for your children. Perhaps your children participate in sports or take piano lessons. Encourage them to continue with their normal routines. You can probably find a friend who would be willing to videotape their activities so that you can still be a part of their lives. If you help with your children's homework, you could continue to do that from your hospital bed. Arrange for them to come with their books at your best times—after medication and rest, when you feel your best and are alert. That could also be a good time for your spouse to do household chores or to have what is probably much-needed time alone.

Those times could present wonderful opportunities for your children to voice questions or concerns about what is happening to you, something that could make them more comfortable with death and greatly benefit them throughout their lives.

On the other hand, while there should be openness to talk about your impending death, it doesn't always have to be the foremost thought in your minds. Your family won't have any problem remembering your situation; in fact, they are more likely to need your help to forget it occasionally. The most important goal is to continue to make warm, special memories for your loved ones to cherish after you're gone.

Visiting Hours

Even though it is important for you to be open with loved ones and to allow others to share this time with you, you also need to take responsibility for being alone when you need to be. At first, you may find that you will welcome everyone who comes to visit. You feel reasonably well, and you're grateful that they cared enough to come.

As your health begins to deteriorate, you will find fewer visitors showing up. You may be grateful for that, or you may resent it. Try not to be too hard on them. Many people feel uncomfortable in the presence of someone who is dying. It isn't that your friends care less—they probably just don't know what to say. Perhaps they want to give you the privacy they feel you need, or maybe they think you need to reserve your strength for your immediate family. When they do come, their visits will come farther apart and be shorter. Most likely, you will appreciate their short visits and will even begin to narrow the field of people you wish to have present for more than a few minutes.

A hospital room is often regarded as public property, a place where people come and go without invitation. Feel free to ask guests to wait in the lounge until you feel like seeing them. If you can't do this yourself, ask your spouse or another family member to address the situation for you. This is your space, and, within reason, you can control who comes and how long the person stays. It can be a challenge to do that without bruising a few feelings, but sometimes you will need to. As time goes on, you will want to see a smaller number of people, and the relationships you do retain will be more intense.

A Circle of Friends

The closer you get to death, the more you will need those special friends to help you through this process, and the more you will appreciate them being there for you.

I knew a young woman named Debbie, the mother of two small children, who requested—and received—the best possible support anyone could hope for in her final months of life.

Debbie and her husband were friends with two other young couples. They belonged to the same service club, spent holidays together, and their children played well together. The three women were particularly close.

One day Debbie had to undergo some tests and x-rays to determine why she hadn't been feeling well. She was diagnosed with terminal cancer.

Immediately, Debbie went to these two friends. They agreed to be available for anything she might need, twenty-four hours a day, as long as she lived. And they followed through on that commitment many, many times in the months to come. Both women arranged their family, work, and vacation schedules around Debbie's needs.

Their assistance took practical forms, like Christmas shopping or taking care of the kids, but Debbie needed them mostly for spiritual and emotional support, often just to talk for hours at a time. In fact, one of her friends was nicknamed "Jaws" because of the number of hours she spent talking with Debbie on the phone!

Debbie's diagnosis was made in early September, and as Christmas approached, she began to weaken. Her friends took her to do her own Christmas shopping, entertained friends with her on Christmas Eve, and helped her reach her goal of staying with the family until after Christmas. Debbie was able to write a note of thanks to each person who had helped her during her illness, including her mother, brother, husband, children, and, of course, her two special friends. She even wrote instructions for her own funeral, to be distributed after her death. After Christmas, Debbie was taken to the hospital and slipped into a coma. She died the day after New Year's.

Debbie's friends were above average in loyalty. Few of us can expect that kind of attention and devotion as we prepare to leave this world. But if you give your family and friends a chance, they may surprise you.

This Is Your Life

This is your life and your death, and it is your choice with whom you share it. But share it with someone—if not for your own sake, then for the sake of the loved ones you may be leaving behind. Nothing has ever affected you so profoundly as facing your own death, and you will have reactions that will shock you.

For a time, intense anger, frustration, and loneliness will affect the way you relate to others. Your family may never have witnessed this side of you. At the same time, you may see a side to them that you have never seen before. Try to remember that your loved ones are experiencing some of the same feelings you are. They, too, are threatened with a huge loss over which they have no control.

Be as honest as you can with each other. Let your loved

ones into the places inside you that are hurting the most. The overwhelming fears and feelings will lose some of their power when they are released from the deep, hidden places within.

two

PROVIDING FOR YOUR PHYSICAL NEEDS

Some animals seem to have an instinct about dying. They know when it's their time. It is thought that elephants will trudge long distances to come to rest at "graveyards" where others have died before them. And dogs that have been seriously injured may look for a quiet place, waiting for healing or the approach of death.

Usually it's different for humans. Even though we all know we're going to die sometime, we're rarely ready for that sometime to be now. We will often make unrealistic promises to God and ourselves about how we will handle life if we ever get through this crisis. Occasionally, though, I have seen a person who accepted death as part of life and took responsibility to prepare for it. By doing so that person avoided an unnecessary measure of pain and discomfort.

At other times in my experience as a caregiver, I have heard hurt and disappointed people say things like, "No one asked if I needed help," "I wouldn't want to bother anyone," or "I don't know anyone well enough to ask for help." Committed friends will try their best to guess your every need, but you can help them by actively participating in creating an environment that is pain-free and comfortable for yourself. Don't be afraid to tell someone when and where you hurt, when you need attention, or when you might be in need of human touch.

In this chapter we will look at four areas where you can have some measure of control, to better prepare yourself physically and emotionally for your final months: relief of pain, nursing care, nutrition, and physiotherapy.

Pain Control

Much of our fear of dying is linked with the anticipation of physical pain and suffering. Years ago, this would have been a more valid concern. Either no medication was available, or it was given on a specified schedule—for example, every four hours, without regard for the intensity of the pain. This practice may have been based on fears of addiction, but it still caused frustration and the feeling of being out of control.

With today's medical practices, no one need die in physical pain. Whether your final weeks are spent at home or in a hospital, you should be able to control your own pain medication. One method is the use of a medicine pump that can flow continuously—or at your option—based on need. Your doctor will determine the dosage. A visiting nurse will take care of and refill the pump.

You may find yourself coming up with plenty of valid reasons to avoid taking pain medication. It can make you lethargic or less alert when you want to be at your best. I have seen patients resist treatment in a subconscious attempt to get attention or as a way of punishing or manipulating family and friends. Deep down, perhaps it was an attempt to hasten the dying process. It's easy to understand that urge to maintain control over one's own life and death. Unfortunately, chances are that death will not hurry, and without medication your final months will just be unnecessarily miserable.

That feeling of being out of control can also cause mental and emotional pain. For possibly the first time since infancy, you won't be able to control your own bodily functions. You may always have been a tidy, well-groomed person, and suddenly you won't even be able to take a shower. Perhaps you are paralyzed, and, try as you might, you can't lift an arm or a leg or even utter a simple thank-you to those who are doing so much for you. Worst of all, death has forced you into a corner. You feel trapped and there is no way out.

At the same time, you have the struggles that come with your changing life and relationships. You might worry about being an emotional and financial burden on your family, yet you have no other options. Most troublesome of all is the unanswerable question of "Why?" *Why is this happening to me?*

The quickest way to emotional and mental relief is to embrace the fact that there are some things you simply cannot change. Acceptance is your medicine, and you will need many doses of it as the end of your life draws near.

On the other hand, as long as you are lucid, you *can* do something about any *spiritual* pain and confusion you may have. If you haven't already done so, now is the time to examine your own beliefs about death. You may even find yourself questioning your whole belief system. It can be painful to realize that you have come to this crisis without having decided for yourself what you believe about some of life's most basic spiritual questions.

What will happen to you when you die? Is there life after death? Where will you spend eternity? It is never too late to voice these questions. Ask a friend, pastor, or advisor whose spirituality you trust and respect to help you search for answers.

A woman in my prayer group called me one day saying she needed to bring her secretary over immediately. Within the hour, my friend and Jean—a petite, well-dressed, alert woman in her early fifties—were seated in my office. This was not a time for small talk, so I asked Jean, "What would you like me to do for you?"

"I'm dying and I don't want to go to hell," she said matter-of-factly. "I want you to teach me about God."

Jean's church attendance as a child had been sporadic and, as an adult, nonexistent. She wanted to know the story of God as related in the Bible. After learning about Abraham, Moses, and David, whose actions did not always please God, she realized, "If God still loved them, then I guess I, too, am acceptable to him." Before following through on most of her final projects she would ask, "Do you think God would be unhappy with me for that?"

I noticed an immense change in Jean, especially in her relationships, after we began to explore the concepts of love and forgiveness in the New Testament. She began trusting her husband to do things she had never allowed him to do before. Unlike her old self, she would call her sisters just to talk. Jean took the initiative to ease her own spiritual pain and confusion, making her final weeks happier and more contented.

The goal is to be in sync: physically, mentally, emotionally, and spiritually. Pain in any one of those areas will increase the pain in each of them. Relieving pain or stress in one brings a measure of relief in all.

Nursing Care

Whether you spend your final days at home or in the hospital, you don't want to leave your nursing care to chance. Your comfort can be greatly affected by the skill and attitude of those caring for you. In some situations you will not have much control over the nursing staff. In others, the choice is completely yours.

If you are in a hospital you can be confident that you are in the hands of qualified medical professionals. But skill alone isn't everything. What you don't need is a nurse who cannot accept death or who has an unrealistic determination to make you well. You need someone who is compassionate and whose goal is to make you comfortable.

Also, it is possible to have a nurse with whom you just don't get along or who has an unfavorable attitude toward you. That could be the case for many reasons, including something personal he or she is going through that has nothing to do with you. For whatever reason, if you find yourself reacting negatively when your nurse enters the room, you have a problem that might require some action on your part. Ask yourself honestly if your own attitude is causing the conflict. If you are satisfied that it isn't, then talk to the head nurse about your options.

If your last days are spent at home, you will need family members and friends around who have more than good intentions. First, they should be comfortable with the reality of death. If being near a dying person is awkward for the ones caring for you, you will feel awkward, too. Also, you will need trained nursing care. Hospices and other health organizations will send representatives to your home to train family members in how to care for you. You still need to be under the supervision of your doctor, but the more training your family can get, the better it will be for everyone involved.

At some point you will need to decide whether you want your last weeks and days to be spent at home or in a hospital. That decision is so important that hospice organizations and home-nursing providers have guidelines for families considering the possibility of a loved one dying at home. Should you decide to stay at home, you could benefit from contacting such an organization in your area. Before you do that, though, here are some basic questions to consider as you make your decision:

1. Is your attending physician willing to remain supportive and involved with you at home?

2. Do both you and your family have a sincere desire that death take place at home?

3. Do you and your family have the physical, emotional, and financial ability to provide adequate care at home?

4. Do you and your family understand that, at any time, unforeseen complications may require hospitalization, pre-empting your desire to die at home?

All family members and friends who will be involved in caring for you should understand the physical, emotional, and spiritual energy that will be required of them. In most of the cases I have seen, the family considered it well worth the effort.

Lorne, a seventy-eight-year-old man with a malignant lung tumor, had six months to live. Having been sick with other ailments for many years, he felt he'd had enough of hospitals. He begged his wife, "Please don't leave me in the hospital to die. I want to die at home."

Even though Lorne had never been an easy patient to care for, his wife of fifty-eight years agreed to do everything she could to allow him to die at home. The dining room furniture was moved to the basement, and the open dining area became Lorne's room. The living room couch became his wife's bed.

The couple's six children were eager to help, especially in giving support to their mother. Several of the children lived in the immediate area and were always available. One daughter who lived two hours away came to be with the family every weekend. Another daughter rearranged her schedule to have four days off every two weeks. Although there were some things, like bathing or inserting a catheter, that Lorne's modesty wouldn't allow his children to do for him, they all cared for their father through the training and supervision of a home-care nursing program.

The family doctor agreed to be available to supervise medication and the visiting nurses, and every week a homemaker came to clean the house. Lorne's wife's main responsibility was to feed the steady stream of people who came to be with him.

Because of his family's commitment, Lorne spent his last months as a center of activity and attention, rather than "tucked away" upstairs. He was able to greet guests, as he had always done, until his final day. Lorne died, as he wanted to, at home with his wife and children by his side.

Not everyone will have a large family or one that, for valid reasons, can be available and supportive to such an extent. But if you prefer not to die in a hospital, you still have other options. All over the country, hospice organizations offer kind, compassionate, and quality nursing care to the dying. There is no fee for hospice services, and a doctor's referral is not necessary. Usually, hospices provide social workers, nurses, and clergy from all denominations. Nonprofessional volunteers play a key role in supporting patients and their families in the hospital or at home. Hospice nurses and caregivers regularly help many dying persons' final weeks be comfortable and peaceful.

Nutrition

Your diet—what you eat, or, more importantly, what you don't eat—will greatly affect your physical comfort in your final weeks. You can't be comfortable when your stomach is empty. One problem is that seriously ill people may not know when they are hungry. Hunger pangs can feel just like the pain of an illness or be so similar that it is hard to tell the difference.

Medication can't take away hunger pangs, so if you have been given pain medicine but still feel uncomfortable, it could be because you need food in your stomach.

It is best to eat regularly, whether you feel hungry and ready to eat or not. Try to have appealing food that agrees with your stomach available at all times. This will be harder to do if you are in a hospital but won't be impossible. See if a friend or family member can regularly bring food that you like or are craving.

If you are no longer able to eat solid foods, you can get prepackaged liquid meals through a drugstore or home care nursing program. You won't enjoy them like you would a gourmet meal, but they will provide a high protein diet with all the nutrition you need to help keep you feeling full and comfortable in your final days.

One thing you will need to guard against is the temptation to use food as a means to an end. I have seen patients refuse food—as they did medication—in the hopes of ending their lives sooner, in order to get sympathy, or as a way of manipulating family or friends.

I knew a woman named Joyce who lay in a hospital room dying from a terminal illness. She demanded that her son be at her side every moment, and she refused to eat or even take a sip of water unless he gave it to her. Joyce was perfectly capable of taking fluids, but her health deteriorated because she wouldn't. Soon she had an IV in her arm to keep her from dehydrating.

Not only did Joyce's health decline, but so did her relationship with her son. Eventually, repulsed by her clinging and manipulation, he could only tolerate her presence for a few moments at a time.

Joyce lived a miserable life because she was angry with the world and everyone in it. She used her razor-sharp tongue to hurt and humiliate the people trying hardest to love her. Just as in her life, Joyce's attitude made her death miserable for herself and everyone with whom she came in contact.

Most patients who use food as a means of control are totally unaware of what they are doing. If confronted, they would deny it. You can guard against doing this, even subconsciously, by being aware of how easily it can happen. You can also give a close family member or friend permission to help you recognize that tendency in yourself.

Physiotherapy

The thought of physiotherapy brings to mind extensive treatment by a professional physiotherapist, with all kinds of high-tech gadgets for treating damaged muscles. That could be required (depending on your situation), but you have another condition that calls for a different kind of attention. This probably isn't a conscious need, and most people wouldn't think to request treatment for it, but it is a crucial reality for every human being: "skin hunger."

Your comfort and sense of well-being can be greatly enhanced by frequent touching from loved ones. You may just need your face wiped with a damp, cool cloth, or someone may need to "exercise" for you by moving your arms and legs and gently massaging your muscles. It's important to optimize circulation to your limbs as a way of discouraging the development of bed sores. Also, frequent turning and light coughing can help prevent pneumonia, a common occurrence in bed-ridden people.

If it is painful to be moved, light stroking of the skin can be soothing and comforting. But even if it hurts, human touch is vital to your physical and emotional well-being. Your spouse is the most logical person to whom you can express your need for touch.

More specifically, you and your spouse's sexual needs do not go away just because you are ill. In fact, the emotional crisis of your impending death could create a closer bond, increasing your desire for physical and emotional intimacy. You and your partner's desires should be honored as far as possible and practical, as long as you live.

Unattractive scars, or even impotency, need not end sexual activity. Don't assume that your spouse is turned off by any physical changes that have occurred. Try to be open with each other about your fears and insecurities. And don't be embarrassed to talk to your doctor, pastor, or anyone else you trust who might be able to offer creative and mutually satisfying solutions to your sexual difficulties.

Taking the initiative to act on the areas of pain control, nursing care, nutrition, and physiotherapy can be difficult. But once you take responsibility for your own comfort, you will feel less like a victim and more in control of your own life and death.

three

MAKING PROVISION FOR LOVED ONES

A few years ago an older man signed his farm over to his son with the verbal proviso that the man and his wife could live on the farm until their death. He left his only other assets, a few thousand dollars in cash, in equal shares to his wife and their four grown and financially secure daughters.

Unlike the mother, the man got along well with his son. He probably never could have imagined that after his own death, his son and daughter-in-law would evict his wife from her home, leaving her with no support except the welfare system. One daughter kindly signed over her share of the inheritance to her mother, but the other three said, "No, this is the way Dad wanted it."

Actually, it *wasn't* how Dad had wanted it. He never intended to leave his wife with no money and no place to live. He thought he had provided for her until her death, but because he didn't put the arrangements in a will, his wife and family are still suffering the consequences. The brother and the sisters aren't speaking to each other, the cousins aren't allowed to play together, and a woman has been deprived of the companionship of her children and grandchildren.

Eventually, the widow won a court settlement that allowed her to live modestly, but if her husband had sought legal advice on how to properly provide for her after his death, she would have been spared that humiliating and painful experience.

The majority of people I have known who were dying had a deep concern for the physical and emotional well-being of loved ones they would be leaving behind. Many of them went to extraordinary lengths before death to ensure ongoing care for their families. Some arranged for this in a will, and others thought they had provided for their loved ones, when in fact they had not.

Perhaps certain people come to mind as you contemplate the time when you will be gone. Some of them may be totally dependent on you, such as children, siblings, or aging parents. Others may be friends who enjoy and appreciate their relationship with you and will miss your presence in their lives. You can take steps now to provide for those loved ones who depend on you and to make meaningful memories with special friends.

You Need a Will

Fifty to a hundred years ago, the typical pattern was that Mom and Dad stayed married for life and groomed their children to take over the family farm. The grandparents lived nearby until one of them died, and then the surviving grandparent moved in with the family, to be cared for until death. Almost everyone could be assured of at least some security in old age.

Unfortunately, it seldom happens this neatly today. Divorce commonly breaks up families, children move across the country (if not across the world), and family businesses are much fewer in number. Without an adequate will (and sometimes even when there is one), legal disputes over who is entitled to what can cause hurt feelings and division that may last for years.

You can help your family avoid this kind of painful conflict by deciding for yourself who will inherit your possessions. Younger or older, single or married, childrearing or childless, you should have an updated will, especially if you know you are approaching the end of your life.

The following general guidelines are things you need to know about having, and not having, a will. Laws vary according to state or province, so these guidelines cannot replace the advice that you will need to get from an attorney about your specific situation.

- A will cannot be written unless the person is of sound mind. An attorney and attending physician determine if a dying person is under the influence of medication to such an extent as to place the soundness of mind in doubt.

- A will is valid if it can be written and signed in the person's own handwriting. No witnesses are required.

- If a will has not been written and the person is unable to write one, the estate will go to the surviving heirs, not to the government. However, in most cases it will first have to go through probate court.

- If a person dies without a will, the spouse has the right to inherit the estate after application to the court. The order of inheritance is spouse, child(ren), parents, siblings, and other relations, either by blood or legal adoption.

If you are young and can't see any reason for having a will, ask an attorney's advice. You might be surprised at the many good reasons there are for a person of your age and status to have a will.

Ours is a death-denying society, where the feeling persists that the act of preparing a will can precipitate death. People often put off making a will, as if that will help prevent death, when in reality it only makes life more difficult for the family members left behind.

While you can't guarantee that complications won't arise after your death, you can do your best to leave no room for other family members to contest the will. This allows your spouse and children to grieve your death and get back to daily life as soon as possible. Contesting a will puts the grieving process on hold and can create much confusion and hurt, no matter what the outcome.

Many long court battles have been fought over what seemed obvious to one person but not to others. If you make decisions ahead of time about the distribution of your possessions, and work with a competent attorney, you will be taking good care—both emotionally and physically—of the people you love the most.

Family First

Your first financial responsibility is to your spouse and dependent children. A good will is one in which all your possessions are bequeathed to your partner. When children are involved, ideally there would be a joint will that covers three different contingencies: (1) the husband's death prior to the wife's (with his estate going to her), (2) the wife's death prior to the husband's (with her estate going to him), and (3) the simultaneous death of husband and wife (with both of their estates going to their children, the naming of an executor and a trustee for the combined estate, and the designation of a guardian for the children).

A few generations ago, the guardian probably would have been one of the godparents named at birth by the children's parents. Godparents were to contribute to the spiritual growth of their godchildren, and would become foster parents if both parents died. Unfortunately, the concept of godparenting has largely been lost in our society. Today, even when single parenting is so common, we often leave our children's care to chance. We owe them so much more than that.

If your children are old enough to comprehend death, they are old enough to be told of your impending death and your plans for their welfare. In fact, you might be surprised at the insights and input children can offer concerning their own continuing care.

You should also keep the role of grandparents in mind when determining your children's future. Grandparents have no automatic legal rights to custody or access to their grandchildren, although they may apply to the courts for those rights. Usually, grandparents are at the mercy of the will-appointed or court-appointed guardian when it comes to maintaining contact. Severing that relationship could cause an excruciating and damaging loss for the children as well as the grandparents. If you have any say in the matter, try to keep that bond intact. Your parents and your children need each other, both physically and emotionally, after your death.

When Your Parents Outlive You

Keep in mind that, apart from their relationship with your children, your parents need special attention at this time. In our society of advanced health care, many elderly parents live for years after their children have died in middle age from accidents or terminal illnesses. I have noticed that in such cases the parents' grief is extremely intense. This is partly due to the pain of losing a child, but also to the fact that parents are about fourth in line when it comes to receiving care and condolences from family members and friends.

I remember the funeral of a very popular middle-aged man. His eighty-five-year-old mother sat in a corner of the room watching visitors console her son's widow and their children.

Visibly upset when I approached her, she almost shouted, "Everyone forgets that he was my son!"

While you still have time, you can help compensate for the lack of attention your parents will receive after your death. Perhaps you could give them an item that has been significant in your relationship, such as a favorite gift that they gave you when you went away to college or when you set up your first home. With just a little extra thought, you can help ease your parents' grief in ways that are meaningful to all concerned.

Adults Who Depend on You

Apart from your wife, children, and parents, you may be concerned about other loved ones, such as elderly or handicapped adults who depend on you for their survival. Your provision for them could include a variety of forms of physical and emotional care.

May was an energetic sixty-year-old when she retired after working for forty years in a small, family-owned company. Just one year later I visited her in the cancer ward of a large hospital. May wasn't concerned about her own death. She said intensely, "I can't die until I know my mentally handicapped brother will be taken care of when I'm gone."

With her doctor's permission, and accompanied by a friend, May went home for a week. I left for ten days, and by the time I returned, May had done everything necessary to provide a secure future for her brother.

Under the guidance and direction of an attorney, May had appointed as guardian a friend who was willing and able to provide Henry with funds from a trust account. This friend was to pay Henry's rent, see that he always had nutritious food, and even take him shopping for clothes. He was taken care of in every way.

May not only provided for Henry's physical well-being, but just as importantly, she succeeded in transferring her brother's affection and allegiance from herself to her friend. May died knowing that Henry would be happy and secure in the loving hands of someone who was as committed to him as she had been. I saw Henry several years after May's death, and the transference of his allegiance to this friend was so complete that he hardly remembered his sister anymore.

In arranging for the care of loved ones who are dependent on you, you will want to do everything you can to prevent panic, confusion, or insecurity when you're gone. Ideally, another relative or close friend will be available and capable of taking over the nurturing of your dependent loved ones.

Making Memories

After you have taken care of your immediate family, you might want to think about how you can help special friends adjust to your impending death. You could leave something for them in your will, such as a prized possession that has meaning for you both. Or, to give your friend a warm memory as well as a gift, consider giving it personally beforehand.

I suggested this to Dorothy, an older woman in my congregation who was dying of lung cancer. She had accumulated many beautiful things over the years, which she wished to give to various friends. After she said several times anxiously, "I hope I've made my wishes clear to my lawyer," I realized the depth of her concern that each person receive the right thing.

When I suggested she give her things to her friends while she was still living, Dorothy was hesitant. She didn't want to make people uncomfortable. Eventually, though, she agreed to try it if the opportunity presented itself. It didn't take long before her chance came.

A woman from the church came to visit her. Dorothy knew her well enough to explain what she wanted to do and her hesitancy. The woman graciously received a lovely reminder of their friendship. Dorothy began inviting her friends over for tea and made a private, meaningful ceremony of giving the gifts she had planned to have her attorney distribute. In so doing, she gave a part of herself in the form of special memories to her friends.

Most people, when they are approaching death, begin to visualize their loved ones owning and using their favorite possessions. A grandmother may see an expensive vase on the mantle of her first granddaughter's home. A father may imagine his son playing golf with his favorite clubs. A woman may realize the new dress she never got to wear would be perfect for her best friend. Imagine how much more meaningful each of those items would be if the grandmother, the father, and the friend gave them away personally. Doing so may also help avoid conflict among your family members after your death.

I should caution you that this idea can be taken to extremes. I'm suggesting that you give away small mementos, such as dishes or jewelry. Don't give so much away that friends and loved ones feel like they're leaving you in an empty house, waiting to die. I heard about an elderly man who kept urging his daughter to go ahead and take the dining room set he was going to leave to her in his will. Even though the daughter knew it was just a matter of time before her father's death, she wouldn't even consider taking the furniture and leaving a big hole in her father's home.

No Surprises

Whatever you do to physically provide for your loved ones will have everything to do with how they cope emotionally after you're gone. For instance, it is critical that you talk about your financial situation with an attorney and your family, particularly your spouse. Leave as few surprises as possible.

I knew a middle-aged couple who purchased a home in the husband's name. They had lived in and enjoyed their home for several years when the husband suddenly became ill and died. A couple of months after the funeral, a man contacted the widow, wanting the past two months' rent payments. When she obviously didn't know what he was talking about, the man informed her that her husband, in desperate need of quick cash, had sold their home. Unbeknown to her, they had been renting from the man for several years.

As long as her husband was healthy and able to pay the rent, his secret was safe. Even when he became ill, he told no one of the transaction. It was a devastating shock for the woman to learn that, instead of owning her own home, she owned a pile of rent receipts. Furthermore, she discovered that her husband's life insurance had lapsed and there was barely enough money to pay his funeral expenses. The widow was understandably furious. Now she had intense anger and bitterness to deal with on top of her grief and all the financial problems her husband had left her.

In this case, the man had done nothing to provide for his wife, physically or emotionally, after his death. Had he talked with her and a financial counselor, they could possibly have worked out a solution that the wife could have afforded, sparing her much trauma.

Think also about the accumulated papers, legal documents, and correspondence that may have been packed away for years in your drawers or filing cabinets. Old property deeds can look like useless papers to the uninformed eye. Advise your family about valuable documents that could accidentally be thrown away when you're gone. You might also want to go through photographs, identifying old family members or school friends whom only you might know.

What about anything that might cause hurt or embarrassment to your family? I knew a woman who married in late middle age. During the courtship, her future husband impressed her family with many exciting tales of his exploits in

World War II. He flew bomber aircraft from Canada over the North Atlantic, braving the antiaircraft fire of enemy patrol boats, and went on to fly many dangerous missions over Germany. The man died shortly after the wedding, and his wife was left to sort through and dispose of his belongings. Military service records showed that he had not been a pilot at all. He had never left his accountant's desk at Air Defense Headquarters in Ottawa.

My advice is to tell the story straight. Don't present yourself as something that you're not, and if there are events in your past that you yourself would just as soon forget, don't hang onto memorabilia or documents that could embarrass your family later.

Keep the surprises to a minimum. After you are gone, your family members will have plenty of other challenges to cope with.

four

GIVING
YOURSELF
AWAY

My mother-in-law, an old-fashioned Newfoundlander, lived in our home for two years. We enjoyed her company immensely, just as we did her delicious, nutritious meals and home-baked bread. Near the end of her stay with us, my husband and children informed me that I would have to be the bread baker in the family after Mom left.

When I asked her to write down her bread recipe, she was surprised that anyone would think to ask for it. Mom grew up cooking and had probably never used a recipe in her entire life. She didn't know what to tell me.

"Okay," I said, "Just tell me what ingredients you use." Another problem. When it came time to bake bread, she always knew what she needed, but otherwise she couldn't really tell me that, either.

Later that afternoon, Mom and I stood in the kitchen, surrounded by measuring spoons, cups, bowls, and every possible bread ingredient I could think of. I was ready with pencil and paper to write down everything I saw, exactly the way she did it. She measured the ingredients with the palm of her hand, adding what she needed to make the mixture feel "right." Of course, her bread turned out as it always did, perfect and delicious.

For the next two weeks, Mom watched and corrected me as I baked bread. The first time, it didn't turn out at all like hers. We altered the recipe, and she analyzed the way I mixed and kneaded it. By the time she left, I was turning out well-rounded, crispy-crusted loaves that filled the house with that special scent of home-baked bread.

Mom died several years later, and we inherited a few of her material possessions. But the most precious treasures I received from her were the skill of baking bread and the joyous memory of doing it together.

The most meaningful legacy you will leave to your loved ones is intangible. It's not your house, your car, or your money. Everything that is material will eventually run down or run out. What will live on with people are the parts of yourself that you give to them—your skills, talents, and interests.

Give a Good Attitude

The most important gift you can leave to your closest family members is a good attitude about your death. Of course, you will struggle with extreme emotions of feeling betrayed, of not understanding, of blaming someone—anyone—for what is happening to you. Your gift to family and friends will be to learn how to feel, and yet control, those emotions instead of letting them control you. If you are angry and bitter about your death, in a sense you will encourage your family to be bitter too. As difficult as it may sound, if you can accept your death and make your remaining time as productive as possible, you will also be helping your loved ones deal more positively with it.

For years to come, you will be remembered by your attitude during this time. If you are kind and considerate toward others, people will always think of you that way and be grateful.

If you are grumpy, demanding, and rude, it will be hard for them to remember you in any other way. No one expects a perfect attitude from you at a time like this. With the pressures that you are under, it's unrealistic to think that you will never react negatively to the situations and people around you. The goal is to be aware of how your attitude is affecting others' feelings. If necessary, ask for forgiveness, but try your best not to leave a legacy of pain for family members and friends to deal with after you're gone.

Personality Conflict

During his final weeks of life, my father gave an intangible gift to his family that has stayed with us for years. He made a conscious decision to act in ways that were contrary to his personality. To make his death as painless as possible for all of us, he made what had to be hard choices: to be congenial, to talk when he really didn't want to, and to let go of his routines.

For example, for many years my father won our city's "yard-of-the-year" award for his beautiful, well-manicured lawn. He was extremely proud of his yard and would never allow anyone else to touch it or help him maintain it. During his final illness, I'm sure my dad's natural tendency would have been to hang on tightly to his ownership of an award-winning yard and to complain about his inability to care for it.

Instead, Dad decided to teach one of his grandsons how to care for the yard exactly as he had done. He watched and directed from the living room window as his grandson tried his best to do what my father had done so well for so many years. Dad was surprised and overjoyed when, once again, his was named "yard-of-the-year."

My dad had also never been much of a talker, especially in terms of one-to-one, intimate conversations. But during his final days I had many long talks with Dad. He wanted to pass on to me, the oldest of his six children, the responsibility he had always carried for the extended family. Those times with him are my favorite memories of Dad. But if he hadn't made a choice that was contrary to his usual reserved personality, I wouldn't have those memories today.

If you are self-assured and outgoing by nature, such special times with family and friends will happen almost automatically. You will know what would be most meaningful for each one, whether it's a skill you teach your daughter, a letter you write to a special friend, or maybe special moments when a child has your undivided attention. If that comes easily for you, then both you and your loved ones are fortunate. But you may be shy or reserved and feel like you have nothing to offer. Like my dad, you have a choice to make. You can control your personality, or you can allow it to control you. It could be risky to reach out to give something of yourself to others. There may be some awkward silences when you don't know *how* to say what you want to say. What if you try to teach a skill to someone who just can't get the hang of it? It's okay. Just by trying, you will have given a special memory.

The key is to find the most comfortable ways for you to reach out to others. If it's hard verbally to express love face-to-face, perhaps you could make a video or audio recording, or share your feelings in a letter.

That's what Alice, a woman who was dying from a terminal illness, did during her last few weeks of life. Before she lost too much weight, she had her picture taken with each child and grandchild. She wanted them to remember her the way they had always known her. Until her death, she kept the pictures on the dresser where she could see them.

When I visited Alice she could tell me, with some prompting, what she loved so much about her children, but the thought of expressing it to them made her uncomfortable. I suggested that she write her feelings about each child on paper.

She liked the idea but was too weak to write, so she dictated her messages to me. We placed the notes behind the backing of the pictures and, after Alice's funeral, her husband gave them to the children. Of course, they knew their mother loved them, but because Alice had never been one to express much emotion, they were surprised at the depth of her feelings. After reading her letter, one daughter asked me, "How much of this is you and how much of it is Mother?" I assured her that I had acted strictly as a secretary and that the words—and the feelings—had come from her mother's heart.

Yes, Alice had been nervous about the idea. It was contrary to her personality. But the important thing is that she did it anyway. Chances are that it was also more comfortable for her children to receive expressions of her love in that form.

Giving Away Talents

Whatever your personality, and whether you realize it or not, you have much to leave your loved ones. Your talents help define who you are and give meaning to your life. Are you a gourmet cook? Have you always made your children's clothes? Do you have carpentry skills to pass on? Let those parts of you live on by teaching them to someone else.

Even if you have no apparent specialized skills, you may have responsibilities that others will have to pick up after you are gone. If your health allows, and if you have the opportunity, try to take the time and effort to teach them what you know, especially the little tricks of the trade you have learned the hard way.

The Wisdom of Youth

If you are young, don't assume that you have nothing to give or that people won't listen to you. Your years, however few, are full of lessons you have learned from life's experiences, lessons that can benefit others.

I knew a thirteen-year-old girl named Tina who was dying of bowel cancer. When the family realized she wasn't going to live until her sister's upcoming wedding, they wanted to postpone it. In spite of her age, Tina realized she could be a positive influence on the family by the way she dealt with her own impending death. Facing the situation with openness and honesty, she convinced her sister to go ahead with her plans. Tina died the day before the wedding.

Her courage helped family members face their own fears and pain about her death. Tina's example encouraged her parents to grieve their daughter's death openly and together. Instead of tearing their marriage apart, as the death of a child can do, her parents' marriage became stronger than ever.

Tina is just one example of the profound truth and amazing courage I have observed in younger persons who knew they were dying. In fact, my own ministry to dying persons was birthed out of the death of an eighteen-year-old cancer victim named Jim.

I had known Jim for a while, and even though our opinions differed on many issues, we had a good friendship. Just before his death, he asked to see me. "I have a gift to give you that will make you a better minister," he said. He spoke honestly about his doctors, nurses, family, and friends who would not give a straight answer to his questions about his condition. He said he started out with questions like, "What is my temperature?" or "What did my last test show?" Later he moved on to the real issue: "Am I going to die?" Jim received vague answers like, "You're doing fine," or "The next series of tests will tell us more." He heard everything but the truth.

Jim knew he was dying. He was frustrated by not being part of the treatment of his own body and angry at being lied to. Finally he confronted his doctor, who told him the truth but followed it up with, "Don't tell your mother that you know." Jim made a decision to dispose of the secrecy, what he called "lopsided triangles," by confronting his mother in the doctor's presence. As the interaction between Jim, his mother, and the doctor increased, much of his anger vanished.

The intensity of this young man's pain at not being dealt with honestly, his commitment to face death head-on, and his advice to me to help people through their dying processes instead of trying to protect them from it, were the gifts that set my ministry on its proper course. Whether you are younger or older, if you give yourself away, your life—and death—can help mold the lives and character of your loved ones.

five

REVIEWING
YOUR
LIFE

As their physical capabilities decrease, an interesting thing often happens to people who are elderly or dying. They become storytellers. As a child, I was happiest when I was listening to my grandfather and uncle trade stories about their child-hood hunting and fishing vacations and about my ancestors. I must have sensed that they appreciated being asked to share their adventures, because they repeated them many times at my request. Unfortunately, as I grew older, my desire to hear their stories lessened, while their need to tell them increased. Eventually, they would recount their escapades to anyone who would listen—or who would politely pretend to.

At the time I didn't know that it is a natural thing for people to mentally or verbally relive their lives as the end draws near. While some intentionally look back to put their lives in order, most are only aware that something is compelling them to think about the past.

The Value of Reviewing Your Life

That almost indefinable "something" is a need for one's life to be validated, to be assured—not by others (although we may need their help), but by our own realization that our life has had meaning and purpose. You may not have had the same level of achievement as others, but reviewing your life isn't about comparisons. It's about looking back at what you started with, seeing how far you have come, and taking care of what Elisabeth Kübler-Ross calls "unfinished business," until we can celebrate the life and love we have shared with others along the way.

For some, who are full of regret, the purpose of such review is to come to the point of accepting and honestly grieving the fact that life has been one big disappointment. I remember one elderly woman who shared with me her pain at never having had children. Her husband had died years earlier, and she was now alone in her old age. She had convinced herself that with children she never would have experienced a moment of loneliness, and she couldn't see any other redeeming features of her life. Even God's grace was not a reality for her. There was nothing to do but help her accept and mourn the fact that the past could not be changed, and to encourage her to think of something positive she was able to accomplish because she *didn't* have children.

People often evaluate their lives on the basis of the bad things they have done or what they feel they should have done, instead of focusing on the positive things that they did accomplish. To make matters worse, sometimes these judgments of themselves are based on untrue statements made by others or on their own flawed perceptions of what really happened. Such festering, painful memories can become more and more detached from the facts as time goes on. One purpose of life review is to help prevent our interpretations of a few negative incidents from overshadowing the positive things that have happened in thirty, fifty, or seventy years of living.

Finishing Business

Our English word *religion* comes from Latin and is derived from the word *religare*, which means to bind together. That is what sharing stories does—it binds us to our past, to God, and to one another. It also prepares us emotionally for our future. Don't be surprised, and don't feel like you're being selfish, if you find yourself wanting to talk about your life. You need to contemplate the past, especially those hurtful, destructive events buried deep in your memory that suddenly start coming to mind. Until these are dealt with, they will continue to influence your attitudes and actions in negative ways.

I'm not suggesting that you wallow in past pain or dredge up events that were dealt with long ago. Life review is not intended to be a time of confession, but of remembering, of looking at things realistically—possibly for the first time. Ask yourself, what would it take to clear your conscience?

Sometimes, after talking to others who shared an experience with you, you will discover that they remember it differently than you do. You misunderstood someone's words or motives or a sequence of events. You discover a missing piece and find, after all this time, that the situation wasn't the way you thought it was at all. That sudden understanding of the way things really happened can be a very liberating revelation.

On the other hand, there could be something that has haunted you for years. You may have known at the time that you were doing something wrong and have regretted it ever since. It could be that you need to make some kind of restitution. Perhaps you need to replace a stolen item or admit that you lied to someone. If circumstances make that impossible, there is still one important thing you can do—forgive yourself. The goal is to get from the negative in your life to the positive as quickly as possible.

Life Review Methods

Over the years I have found several methods that assist the life review process. Not all of them are suited to every person, since they depend on the availability of time and resources. And without much effort you can probably come up with additional methods more suited to your personality or situation.

• *Written or taped autobiographies.* One of the gifts you can give to yourself and your family is to write or tape your life story. It can be as short or long, general or detailed, as you wish. If your health doesn't allow you to handle this project alone, you can probably find eager helpers among your family members who would be willing to write or record as you speak, or interview you to keep the flow of information as concise as possible.

Try to think of some things that you have rarely, or never, told your family, things that they would enjoy passing on to their children and grandchildren. I recently videotaped my eighty-year-old mother and learned, for the first time, things I had never heard concerning her childhood—like how she felt at age eleven, when her mother died, and the paralyzing fear she experienced during a hurricane.

Your tape doesn't need to chronicle your most horrendous experiences. It could just be a collection of stories. Talk about your most embarrassing moment, your first kiss, or your observations of how the world has changed since you were born. If you're younger, your family will enjoy hearing your favorite memories, in your voice, for many years to come.

I sat with a family as they listened to a tape left by their seventy-four-year-old father, who had recently died. They shared the joy of family memories, as well as many tears and deep healing when the father confessed his regret at not having expressed more often the love he felt for his wife and children. The tape drew the family closer together and helped them grieve the loss of a loving father—instead of the reserved man who for so many years had kept himself emotionally separate from everyone else.

● *Pilgrimages.* A seventy-five-year-old friend of mine was invited to return to the Canadian town where he lived as a boy to witness the demolition of the schoolroom he had attended. He said he felt compelled to visit the place of his youth and reestablish contact with other homesteaders he had known forty-five years earlier. It was a rich experience that brought back many long-forgotten memories and feelings. Shortly after the man returned, he learned that he was dying from a terminal illness. That trip to his past had helped prepare him for what lay ahead.

Going back to where you came from, the places of your birth, childhood, or young adulthood, can be the most effective way to ground your life in reality. If you have time to devote to it, you will also appreciate having pictures and notes assembled in an orderly manner to transport you and your family to those places again and again in the months and years to come.

If you can't physically withstand a trip, you can accomplish much the same purpose by contacting long-lost friends through correspondence or by telephone. Reminiscing about your old neighborhood, the corner drug store, or the games you played can be as effective as being there. It may not be as hard as you think to track down people from your past. Try the local post office, the library, or telephone information to find relatives still living in the area.

Pilgrimages often allow the opportunity to sort out some of the inconsistencies in your memory. You may get a more realistic perspective on situations that you remember as being hurtful. Some things will be exactly as you remembered them, and you will realize that others aren't the way you remembered them at all.

• *Reunions.* Family, church, and high school or college reunions can be fun opportunities for reviewing your life. If you are not physically able to attend, you can contact past school friends by letter or telephone. One benefit of reunions is to see where life has taken you in relation to others.

Don't let worries about whether you have achieved as much success as everyone else keep you from attending a reunion. You'll find that values have changed and that what was important at age twenty-one or twenty-two isn't as important today. Values change even more drastically if you know that death may be near, so you may be able to enjoy a reunion without feeling pressured to live up to anyone else's standards.

• *Genealogies.* Older people are usually more interested in their ancestors than young people are. They appreciate finding their place in history among a long line of relatives. Genealogies can also put into perspective the basic fairness of life, revealing a chain of birth and death that continues through the generations. Learning of so many others who have traveled this road before you can make facing death easier.

Tracking your genealogy can be a daunting task, but don't be put off by what you think you won't be able to accomplish. You can trace several generations rather easily through phone books, city and state records, cemeteries, family Bibles, or through other family members or friends. A relative may have already done extensive research on your family's history. If so, you can be sure that they will love to talk about their discoveries in great detail, making your family-tree climbing much easier than you expected.

Any of these methods of review can add a much greater sense of order to your perspective on your life. They provide good opportunities for resolving old problems, making amends, restoring harmony with those who once were close but have drifted away, and checking old memories against reality.

An article in the journal *Geriatrics* once noted, "The success of life review depends on the outcome of the struggle to resolve old issues of resentment, guilt, bitterness, mistrust, dependence, and nihilism. All the truly significant emotional options remain available until the moment of death: love, hate, reconciliation, self-assertion, and self-esteem" (November 1974, "Life-review Therapy: Putting Memories to Work in Individual and Group Psychotherapy," 165–72).

I don't know anyone for whom this was more true than Jean, the woman who asked me to teach her about God before she died. Many times during my ministry to her I asked myself, "Who is the real Jean?" Through the life review process, I found out, and—much to her surprise—so did she!

Jean was born into a family of six children, between two older sisters and two younger sisters. Her only brother was close to her in age. According to Jean's perception, her mother and father were constantly tired from providing the necessities of life for their large family. The two older girls took care of the two younger ones. Jean remembers her brother being the only person who really cared about her or was available to her.

When her brother began making friends with other boys, Jean decided to learn how to do "boy" things. Her brother was flattered by her efforts and insisted that if his friends wanted to be with him, they had to accept her. That set the pattern for Jean's relationships throughout her life. In every situation, she determined what she needed to do in order to be accepted, and then she did it perfectly. If it became obvious that the other person was not responding, Jean stopped trying and moved on to the next challenge. Her efforts paid off, particularly as an adult in the workplace, where she strived for and earned acceptance, respect, and devotion from her colleagues and supervisors.

Unfortunately, the same wasn't true in Jean's family life. She and her husband had lived a financially comfortable life, but they were not particularly happy. They lived together but led largely separate lives, without intimate contact, for nine years before her illness. Although Jean got along well with one son, the same emotional distance separated her from her younger son. When she learned the severity of her illness, he came to visit with his wife and five-year-old daughter. But Jean didn't appear to be unhappy to see them leave.

True to form, toward the end of her life, Jean determined to do everything possible to die "perfectly." She convinced her husband to buy her dream house, and she became obsessed with decorating it with just the right furniture and the perfect accent pieces. The house was beautiful, yet I couldn't help but feel that Jean wasn't doing the really important things that would help her prepare to die.

One day when I visited, she was extremely upset, precariously pacing the floor with the help of her cane. She couldn't tell me why she was so upset, because she didn't really know. From her barely audible, mumbled comments, it appeared that she was unhappy with herself in some way.

I could tell she was tiring, so I volunteered to leave. But she said, "No. I've got to lie down, but I want you here."

We situated her comfortably in bed, and then I asked, "What has brought you to this point, Jean? Do you want to talk about who you are?"

She waved her hand and yelled, "All this c—p around here—that's who I am!"

Then we talked about her life—about her parents, who had been too tired to care for her, her extreme efforts to win others' approval, and the family she had kept at a distance because they had disappointed her so deeply. And for the first time in the nine years since his death, Jean grieved over the loss of her brother, the one person she believed truly loved and cared for her.

Now that death was near, Jean suddenly understood, for the first time, the truth about the perfectionism that had so controlled her life. Her drive to be the perfect employee, the perfect friend, and even to leave the perfect home for her husband, had all been her way of protecting herself from hurt and from seeing what she now saw—that what is truly important is loving relationships.

When Jean allowed herself to look back on and deal with the past, her priorities changed, her relationships began to mend, and, for the first time in her life, she began to feel really good about herself.

Achieving this kind of realistic perspective and inner peace is the ultimate purpose of life review.

six

LETTING GO

Night after night, a man had the same nightmare: an enormous monster would chase him until he was completely exhausted. Just about the time the monster caught up to him, the man would awaken, trembling with fear.

One night he didn't wake up in time. The hideous creature caught him and held him in its clutches, its foul breath almost suffocating him. In sheer panic, he looked into the monster's face and screamed, "What are you going to do with me?"

The monster replied, "I don't know. It's your dream."

•   •   •

If you sense (or your doctor has told you) that death is close at hand, you may have feelings like those of the man in this story. A creature named death is chasing you and will probably soon catch you. The difference is that this is not a nightmare—it's your life.

Our natural human response is to run away in fear. But, like the man with the nightmare, we can also turn, look the monster in the face, and discover that we are—or can be—in control. Ironically, we gain a measure of control over death by letting go of our feeling that we have a "right" to live, and by giving both our life and our death over to God.

When to Control, When to Let Go

This may sound like a contradiction to what I have said in previous chapters. In every area—from finding someone to share your fears, to reviewing your life—I have encouraged you to take control in preparing for your own death. Now I'm suggesting that you let go. I don't mean that you should let go of your responsibility to face death honestly, to ensure your own comfort, or to provide for your loved ones; if you take control in those areas, your remaining days will be more peaceful and you will leave your loved ones a legacy of dying with grace and dignity. But in most cases, before you will be willing to face those responsibilities, you will have to let go of the need to control when and how you die.

In my years of ministering to dying persons, I have seldom seen people succeed in letting go as a result of an easy, one-time decision. Occasionally, an individual possesses a deep inner peace that death itself cannot disturb. But even that person will go through the natural, healthy progression of fighting an attacking illness, and either beating it or coming to the point of accepting that the disease has won. In other words, there's an inner instinct that says it's time to quit fighting.

I have recently been with a friend who has been told that her illness is probably terminal. She asked me, "When will I know if the treatment is working or not? When do I stop fighting it and accept the fact that I'm dying?"

I told her, "Just never stop being the person you are. Keep walking, and at some point you'll know. Somehow, circumstances will take you from living life as you've known it to the realization that you are in the process of dying. When that happens, open yourself up to people you'd like to have walk through this with you."

What astounded me was the ease with which she was able to ask, "When do I accept this?" Normally, acceptance is a difficult and gradual process in which our fists, clenched so tightly to life, loosen—one finger at a time—until eventually we have let go. I have come to know the process well, not only from helping others go through it, but also by having faced life-threatening illnesses myself.

The first occurred when I was thirty-nine. With four young children, the youngest of whom was ten months old, I was actively involved in life. Then I suffered a stroke that partially paralyzed my left side. As I lay in bed, all I could think about was how much my young family needed me, yet I couldn't even walk or talk understandably. No longer could I be active in my church, in youth organizations, or in the family business. Suddenly I was utterly dependent on others to do for me all the things that had given my life meaning.

Day after day, I fretted over my helplessness. Then a wise woman in the hospital bed next to mine said something that changed my life. She told me, "If you don't get realistic, you're going to make yourself sicker and, if you get home at all, you won't be well enough to straighten out all the things that are going to need to be straightened out when you get there!"

Through this woman's encouragement, I began to see the destructiveness of hanging onto living my life the way I had always lived it. After several soul-searching days, I learned to let go and allow God, the doctors, and my husband to control my life—in my illness, at home, and in the business. Had I learned to let go sooner, my recovery might have been faster.

Another illness occurred just after my sixtieth birthday. It happened during a time of great distress in my life. I had been devastated by the deaths of three people I loved very much. Within a few weeks, someone else I dearly loved attacked my integrity. It was more than my system could handle. I found myself in the hospital's coronary care unit, surrounded by beeping machines with flashing green and red lights.

By this time I had learned, to a great extent, to give control of my life over to God and to those who cared for me. I remember being surprised as I lay on the bed, feeling at peace with whatever was going to happen to me. I had no doubt that God, who had seen me through so many other traumas, was present now. If this was God's time for me to die, I was ready and content to let go. Five days later, the doctor released me from the hospital, with strict instructions and an appointment to return for further tests. Instead of fighting against a specific routine of diet, exercise, and rest, I relaxed and went with it.

The hardest thing was to allow others to clean my house, mow my lawn, and drive my car. Now, even though I'm healthy, I have let go of those things to such an extent that I hire someone to clean my house, and a friend regularly helps me with the yard. I have learned that there are more important things in life than being in control!

I'm not suggesting that if you let go, you will be healed. It may happen, but then again it may not. What I am saying is that if you let go of your life and your death, you will be prepared to "die well."

Why Can't We Let Go?

Through years of experience, I have learned how to tell almost at a glance if a dying person is struggling with issues of control. Usually there is a tendency to push others away, a tense, guarded expression, physical nervousness, and mental confusion. There is much symbolism in the fists that literally clench and unclench in the struggle for control.

One woman in my parish had always had trouble letting people into her life. The possibility that death was approaching only magnified her need to maintain control in every circumstance. I asked her to explain as candidly as possible what it felt like, physically and emotionally, when she thought she might be losing control. She said that she felt physically weak and even got a queasy feeling in the pit of her stomach. Her mind played tricks on her to the extent that she didn't know where she was going or how to get there. She was particularly concerned with what people would think. She had always appeared to be so strong; if she let people know she was dying, they might think she was playing on their sympathies, or they might come to help. And that was something she had never let others do.

This woman had so much fear of losing control that it was even difficult for her to let God get too close, though that was her greatest desire. Yet, like anyone else in a time of crisis, she didn't have the strength to carry through on her own. Some people can ask for help and not feel threatened, but she was not yet able to do so.

Eventually, my friend learned why she had such a hard time letting go. There have been any number of reasons, some perfectly normal and healthy, others decidedly unhealthy. Here are some of the reasons why people resist letting go.

Goals they want to reach. I wish we all fit into the category of people who cling tightly to life because they love it so much. I met a woman who learned she was dying but who just wasn't ready because she wanted to live long enough to see her son and daughter-in-law have a child. Then, of course, she wanted to see that child graduate from college, get married, and have children. To miss those joyous milestones in life would be sad for her as well as for her children and grandchildren. It's understandable that she would try to maintain her grasp on what looked to be such a fulfilling future.

Who would want to end a full and rich life? There are hobbies to pursue, trips to take, books to read, things to learn, people to love. I can't think of a healthier reason to resist death.

Goals they will never reach. Other people hold on tightly because they can't accept the fact that some of their life dreams will never be fulfilled. The disappointment is too great to say "never." They can't bring themselves to say or even think, "I'll never build the business I wanted to own," "I'll never be a wife and mother," or "I'll never have my dream house." Deep down, they know it's true, but it's still hard to say, "Okay, I give up." Yet until they do, they won't be prepared to "die well."

The need to always be in control. People who have always controlled or attempted to control every person, circumstance, and detail around them aren't likely to let death come and take them without a struggle. Their existence has probably always been validated by the level of control they have been able to maintain, and they are determined to keep that control, especially when facing the ultimate threat, death.

As death draws nearer, such "controllers" usually find themselves clinging to one person—maybe a spouse, son, daughter, or close friend—to whom they have slightly opened their hearts. That person becomes a symbolic lifeline. But no one can or should have to live up to that kind of expectation from another. If you see this tendency in yourself, ask someone to help you open up to others who can face death with you.

An absence of stable relationships. During the years of my ministry I have worked with two people who, until the moment they died, desperately clung to their "right" to live, their right to refuse to admit they were dying, and their right to keep all their hostile defenses firmly in place—just as they had always done. When it came to the end, they died entirely alone, having kept an emotionally safe distance from everyone who had ever tried to love and care for them, including God. Those are two of the saddest deaths I ever witnessed.

Human beings were never meant to live as single entities, separated from God and from stable relationships with each other. And they were certainly never meant to die that way. Usually, people begin to shed their emotional armor when they learn that death is approaching. Suddenly they realize, "I'm going to die all alone." And so they begin to ask themselves why they don't have someone to share the end of their lives with. Their fear of dying alone overrides their fear of experiencing more emotional pain, which is what led them to raise their armor in the first place. Slowly, they choose to lower their defenses. But it is a choice, one that no one can make for another.

Unfinished business. In an earlier chapter I referred to May, who was dying of cancer, but who first wanted to make arrangements for her mentally handicapped brother Henry. May took good care of her brother, but one night I discovered that *she* needed taking care of, too. She spoke of her childhood and how, as early as four or five years of age, she was told to get her mother quickly if Henry misbehaved. May was rarely allowed to play with her friends after school, because her mother needed a rest from caring for her brother. For the same reason, she couldn't go to business college in another city. After she completed a local bookkeeping course, within walking distance of her home, she accepted the position that she held for forty years.

During most of her working life, May felt that people in the company took her for granted. As her sixtieth birthday approached, she knew that if she didn't retire, she would never accomplish anything she wanted to in life. May's employer offered many incentives to stay, but she remained adamant about retiring.

May was tired, so she decided to rest. She would spend the summer working in her garden and the coming winter in Florida. But it was not to be. Within six months, she became ill. Tests, x-rays, and surgery revealed that death was near.

One night May began to cry uncontrollably. I held her while she managed to say, "It just isn't fair. I haven't even lived, and here I am dying. No one will even remember that I've been here!"

The next morning, she called and informed me that she was determined to be remembered. She wanted to order a large headstone for her grave, so that people would know she had lived. We ordered the stone that day. Ten days later she died—at peace with herself.

That was May's unfinished business. She needed to grieve the fact that life hadn't been all it could have been for her, and she needed to leave something of herself behind by which to be remembered. Today, visitors at a certain cemetery will see a dignified black marker attesting to May's existence. When she had done these things, she gave herself permission to die, and by doing so, confronted the monster that was threatening her.

A lack of self-acceptance. Accepting ourselves as we are, rather than pretending to be something we are not, is called *congruence*. It means being authentic, or being at one with ourselves. It doesn't help anyone for me to act calm when I'm boiling inside, or to act loving when I'm really feeling hostile. And it gets me nowhere to act confident when I'm scared and unsure of myself. Psychologist Carl Rogers says we must accept our negativeness as a valid part of ourselves. That doesn't mean we have the right to express our negative emotions at the expense of others' feelings, but we must acknowledge them as a legitimate part of our being.

When we are "real"—when we can accept and allow others to see the core of our being, the negative as well as the positive—then we can get on with living as fully as possible for as long as possible.

Letting Go

Every person I know who has faced the prospect of impending death has responded to that realization with clenched fists. The same is probably true for you. Yet even in those clenched fists, you hold the certain knowledge that everyone, including you, will die someday. But up to this point it has all been theory, not reality.

As the numbness begins to dissipate and clarity of mind returns, you will find that your fists are still clenched. You may ask yourself, "How do I let go?" It can't happen by force. People close to you may try to help, saying, "Don't be afraid." But if fear pervades your whole being, you become angry— angry at the person who says, "Don't be afraid," angry at everyone who is healthy, and, mostly, angry at God. As your anger increases, the tension spreads to every muscle in your body. You are so angry—and so afraid of feeling such anger— that even breathing becomes difficult.

Gradually, however, you get to the point of letting go of some small thing, some little bit of anger caused by someone's innocent remark. Or perhaps you let go of some injustice that you had never been able to forgive. Whatever it is that you need to let go of, you make that decision. Slowly, the tension eases. Behind that wound waits another, but you continue the process of clenching and releasing, of hating, then forgiving, of resisting, then accepting, until your hands are wide open and you have completely let go.

seven

CHOOSING
TO
FORGIVE

A young, attractive, Canadian couple in their early thirties lived in a good neighborhood, attended church regularly, and were active in community affairs. The husband was always available to help anyone in need and was the Cub Master of the local Cub Scout troop.

One weekend, during a Scout campout, a nine-year-old boy was discovered missing. A thorough search eventually found him in the woods. The boy had been raped and beaten to death with a rock. The town was stunned and outraged to its core. Who could have done such a hideous thing?

When it appeared that the police were on the verge of identifying him, the killer came forward and confessed. He then killed himself before he could be brought to trial. To everyone's horror, it was the Cub Master.

Many people in that little community refused to forgive the man, or his widow—who was innocent and completely devastated by what her husband had done. Sadly, she even felt shunned by the members of her own church, the ones who should have loved and supported her the most.

But two people did forgive. They expressed concern for the young woman, invited her to their church, and helped her cope with her grief. In one of the most profound displays of Christian love and forgiveness I have ever seen, this couple befriended the widow of the man who had brutally raped and killed their son.

I'm not saying it was easy for them. Any parent would feel anger—even hatred—for the person who did such an unspeakable thing to their child. This couple must have struggled with those emotions. Yet they did the most necessary—and by far the most difficult—thing required of every person who wants to live and die in peace. They chose to forgive.

The Wounds of Life

Fortunately, few of us are called on to forgive someone we know personally for committing such a heinous crime. But almost everyone has had experiences of feeling bruised, or even crushed, by another's actions. Until we deal with the source of those wounds, we will not be able to live life to the fullest, or be fully prepared to die.

Unfortunately, many of us don't even know we have a lack of forgiveness hidden away inside. We are so good at hiding our feelings, especially from ourselves, that we can live for many years without being aware of our invisible wounds. However, others can usually tell that these wounds are there because of the way they affect our actions, attitudes, and health. They can't see the causes, just the effects: explosive tempers, nervous and self-destructive habits, harmful relationships. But they are powerless to ease our pain. Only forgiveness can do that, and no one can force us to forgive. The choice is completely ours.

Before we can make that choice, we have to recognize our lack of forgiveness and its symptoms. The physical results can range from minor nervous gestures or tension, to self-destructive habits, to ulcers or even cancer. Mental or emotional signs could include a "life-has-cheated-me" attitude, an extreme aversion to certain types of people, a volatile temper, or a closed, self-protective countenance. Even if you can't pinpoint a specific unforgiven injury that you have experienced, perhaps you can "diagnose" a lack of forgiveness in yourself from the above symptoms.

I helped a man named Ben deal with hidden anger that he was quite surprised to discover, anger that had festered inside him for years. He was a tall, thin man in his mid-sixties who had never married. For many years, Ben and his older sister, Vera, had shared a home with their mother, a matriarch who ruled her home and children until her death. Ben and Vera were in their late fifties when their mother died.

Ben had been engaged to marry a young woman soon after he returned from active service in World War II. As the wedding date grew near, his mother became ill. The wedding plans were put on hold. His mother never fully recovered, and after several years the engagement was broken.

Day after day, week after week, and year after year, Ben went to work, came home, ate dinner, read the newspaper, and went to bed. On Saturday he looked after the yard, the garage, and the basement. On Sunday he went to church, read a book, and took a nap. That was Ben's life until his mother died.

Then he thought it was his turn to rule the household. But Vera had different plans. She declared, "I am the head of the house now, Ben, or at least an equal partner."

The battle raged for six years.

I met Ben when he entered the hospital with undiagnosed intestinal problems. He wanted a clergyperson who would convince Vera to let him have his way as head of the household. After all, his mother had always gotten her way when *she* was sick. Ben was a good patient when he was hospitalized, but at home he became the demanding, whining individual that he had been prior to hospitalization.

Ben and I spent hours talking about his frustration at living with conflict. The only part of his life he could remember with pleasure was the time spent away from home in military service. As Ben began to realize the depth of his anger, he claimed it was all aimed at Vera, but he couldn't name specific grievances. He was incredulous when I suggested that his mother may have generated a big part of his anger. He couldn't imagine his mother being at fault for anything!

Through our conversations, Ben saw several other things that contributed to his storehouse of anger. One was the fact that his father had been required to cater to his mother's every wish—otherwise she would get sick. Another was a war incident that Ben remembered. In anger, he had killed an enemy soldier when he could possibly have held him as a prisoner of war. Afterward he had made a vow to never again vent his anger. He buried and carried the guilt of that man's death with him until the night we spoke about it so many years later.

Ben grew angry with himself for getting stuck in his mother's and father's molds of manipulating and being manipulated. More than anything, he envied his sister because she had managed to develop her own identity and still be loyal to her parents. He hated her for being everything he wanted to be.

For months I watched Ben struggle to forgive. His life had been wasted and he naturally wanted to blame someone. Eventually, though, he decided that he didn't want to die the way he had lived, frustrated and angry. He realized that he could only find peace by obtaining forgiveness from God, from his sister, and from himself.

Ben requested confession to God and formal absolution, through me, his pastor. He listed his sins on paper, rehearsed them in my presence, and received my assurance of God's pardon. At the same time, he forgave himself.

In the final step, he made an appointment for three hours of his sister's time, asking if I could be present. Almost symbolizing the cleansing he had received from God, Ben wanted to look his best for this meeting. He sat before Vera wearing his nicest suit and with his hair freshly cut. She must have sensed the importance of the situation, because she appeared in a nice dress, with her hair curled and makeup on.

Vera sat near the end of the sofa. Ben was in a nearby chair. The air was thick with tension; Vera's lips were set as if to say, "Tell me what you want, but don't expect anything from me."

Ben began by saying, "I need to talk. Please don't say anything until I'm through." Openly and humbly, he told about some of the incidents in his life that had caused him so much pain.

"Remember my friend, Charles? I really looked up to him and enjoyed his friendship. One time he came to the house and I was so excited. I thought he was coming to see me. When I realized he was there to pick you up for a date, I was devastated."

Ben kept talking, methodically, as if he wanted to be sure there was nothing left for him to feel sorry for. He talked about his regret that his wedding had never happened. For the first time, he began to see his mother's manipulation and that it hadn't been Vera's fault, as he had always believed.

Vera's face softened as Ben continued.

"And remember when I was drafted into the service? Well, I've never told anyone this, but I wasn't drafted. I volunteered because I wanted so desperately to get out of the house."

Tears now spilled from Vera's eyes.

Ben tried to kneel in front of her, but he was too stiff. He sat beside her on the sofa and asked for her forgiveness. They cried together as Vera graciously accepted Ben's apologies and asked his forgiveness for her involvement in their conflicts.

Soon words were no longer necessary. The two held each other until they had cried all their tears. Then Vera dried her eyes, smiled at him, and offered him a cup of tea.

In the following days, the tension in Ben and Vera's home began to dissipate. Ben's need for pain medication lessened by as much as fifty percent, and his mobility increased greatly. He still used his cane, but I noticed with great pleasure a new lightness to his step that stayed with him until his death eighteen months later.

Getting Down to Basics

While forgiving others can be very difficult to do, it is based on such a simple truth—God's forgiveness of us through Christ. Jesus makes forgiveness possible and is our model for forgiving others. He not only taught us to pray, "Forgive us our sins as we forgive those who sin against us," he showed us how to do it.

But it can be hard to know where to begin. In his book *Forgive and Forget* (Harper & Row, 1984, 18) Lewis B. Smedes says there are four stages to forgiveness:

> The pain is so deep you cannot forget—the *Hurt* consumes you and is part of every waking moment. The hurt is gradually covered over by more immediate concerns, however it keeps reappearing at the most inappropriate times. Because it causes so much pain and confusion our lives are disrupted and we *Hate* the person who caused it. No matter how many other good qualities the offender has we cannot wish them well and we want them to suffer as we do. In the normal course of events, God begins to *Heal* our hurt. Unless we are determined to nurse the grudge, the memory of the hurt is healed, we are free and

we are ready to *Come Together.* We invite the person back into our lives. If they come back, healing and restoration are celebrated. If they do not choose to come back you will have to be healed alone.

This "coming together" is known as reconciliation. It's related to—but different from—forgiveness. To *reconcile* means to bring back to friendship after estrangement. It begins when we answer God's urging to forgive someone who has hurt us, or ask someone we have hurt to forgive us. Forgiveness is an act of our will, but reconciliation is a process of growing in love together after forgiveness has been requested and granted.

Are you ready to break free of the pain and loneliness of not forgiving and move on to reconciliation with God and others? Here are some suggestions that may be helpful to you.

Find an advisor. Many people find it helpful to consult a spiritual advisor, someone familiar with the concepts of forgiveness and reconciliation. If you do not know who to ask, consult your doctor, hospital chaplain, or hospice worker. Most clergypersons who work with hospice patients are at ease with interdenominational and interfaith practices. A knowledgeable, compassionate friend may also be an appropriate person to ask for help. What that person does may seem simplistic, but it's a place to start. If a more involved process is needed, then seek out a spiritual advisor with whom you can be thoroughly honest, someone who can give you specific direction and encouragement.

Identify some of the sins in your life. It's tempting to look at yourself and think that, when it comes to sin, you're in pretty good shape—at least compared to some other people you know. When we find ourselves thinking this way, we need to take a second look at God's expectations of us.

The biblical meaning of the word *sin* is to "miss the mark." That "mark" is the high standard of righteousness God sets for us. The Ten Commandments are one place in the Bible where this high standard can be seen (Exodus 20:1-17). Another place is in the gospel of Matthew, where Jesus identifies the two greatest commandments: " 'You shall love the Lord your God with all your heart, and with all your soul, and with all your mind'. . . . [and] 'You shall love your neighbor as yourself' "(22:37-40). Measured against God's standard, all of us fall short of the mark.

As you prepare to take an inventory of your life, here is a list that may help. Consider:

- sins of omission (things you should have done)
- sins of commission (things you did that you shouldn't have done)
- sins of the spoken word
- sins of negative reactions toward others
- pride, impatience, rudeness
- anger, unbelief, and blasphemy against God
- sins of involvement with the occult

Every year on Ash Wednesday, I lead my congregation in a service of penitence, using a checklist based on these areas. The list is by no means exhaustive, but it can provide a place to start checking your own heart.

Examine your conscience by asking yourself the following questions about your relationships with your family, others, yourself, and God. Don't force guilt on yourself. If something comes to mind in one of these areas, write it down. If not, move on to the next one.

- Do I thank God for my family?
- Do I pray for my family?
- Do I thank my family for all they do for me?
- Am I supportive of them? Am I able to ask forgiveness from my spouse and my children and am I able to forgive them?
- Am I kind and patient?
- Do I respect others' integrity?
- Do I like myself?
- Do I use the gifts God has given me?
- Do I ever refuse to exercise my giftedness?
- Do I seek after knowledge of God?
- Do I grieve the Holy Spirit by refusing to follow and listen to God?

If I were standing in front of you now, I would read from Ezekiel 18:30-32: "Therefore I will judge you . . . according to your ways, says the Lord God. Repent and turn from all your transgressions. . . . Cast away from you all the transgressions that you have committed against me, and get yourselves a new heart and a new spirit! . . . Turn, then, and live."

Ask forgiveness from God. Confession and forgiveness are gifts that God has given us to make us whole again. In one sense they are like paint stripper. They clean off the old paint, with its scratches and discoloration, exposing the original wood. But that is only the beginning of the process. Some of the scars we have received in life go deep. Even worse, close examination reveals that at our core is a self-centered nature that, like dry rot, corrupts us from the inside out. A superficial patch-up job just isn't enough. What we need is to be brand-new persons.

The message of the New Testament is that God has provided a fresh start by making it possible for us to share in the death and resurrection of his Son, Jesus: "So if any one is in Christ, there is a new creation; everything has passed away; see, everything has become new! All this is from God, who reconciled us to himself through Christ" (2 Corinthians 5:17-18). Through Jesus, God makes the damaged wood of our lives new again.

When you have confessed to God that you have "missed the mark," and have asked for forgiveness, you can have confidence that God has forgiven you. 1 John 1:9 says, "If we confess our sins, he who is faithful and just will forgive us our sins and cleanse us from all unrighteousness."

Yet if you are anything like me, you also need to hear a human voice—a voice "with skin on"—-assuring you that you have been pardoned. Ask your spiritual advisor to read you a verse from the Bible that affirms this. There are many verses to choose from. A favorite of mine is Micah 7:18: "[God] does not retain his anger forever, because he delights in showing clemency."

Forgive others. You need to forgive anyone whose personal presence or memory causes you anger, anxiety, or fear. Not many people are born into fairy-tale families with two "perfect" parents. Parents are sinful human beings like the rest of us, and their actions can cause deep wounds that may go unacknowledged for years. Siblings also have a way of causing scars that can long go unrecognized. Playmates, school chums, teachers, fellow employees, employers, doctors, children, spouses, and friends—all have played their part, good and bad, in making you who you are. Anyone who has caused you hurt needs to be forgiven.

If you feel it will help, make a list of the persons who have hurt you and write out the incidents that have caused you pain. Don't rationalize or make excuses for the other person's actions, as if you deserved what he or she did to you.

If the experience has crippled your life to any extent, you will need to acknowledge your lack of forgiveness. Cut the strings that hold you in bondage by forgiving those who have hurt you.

You will need discernment to help you decide how to handle each situation. Should you go to the individual involved? Would that person be shocked and hurt to learn that you have been harboring resentment in your heart against him or her? Would it be better to deal with the issue with a neutral party, or has the relationship been damaged in such an obvious way that you need to go directly to the person to make it right? If you don't trust your own judgment to make those decisions, your spiritual advisor should be able to help.

Ask others to forgive you. This will probably be more difficult, since the memories of the wrongs we have done to others are not usually as strong as those of the sins committed against us. If approaching the person will likely cause more problems than it cures, do it privately. For instance, when death is approaching, don't confess a long-past instance of adultery to your spouse; instead, confess it in confidence to a clergyperson and make restitution to your spouse by being faithful, loving, and caring. In the case of lying or slander, confess to the person slandered and all others involved. If you have stolen something, replace it if possible. If not, some form of restitution, as well as confession, is necessary.

Don't let the other person brush off your apology with statements like "It was nothing—forget it." It *was* something—something important enough to weigh heavily on your conscience, and you need to hear the words "I forgive you." Most people are uncomfortable in that situation and don't know what to say, so you may need to be persistent. You may even have to say, "I need to hear you say that you forgive me."

Continue down your list until you feel free of guilt. Don't be surprised if additional incidents come to mind from time to time.

Forgive yourself. There is no need to carry your guilt any more—it is gone. God knows your heart and has forgiven you. Forgive yourself and finish your goal of being healed, of becoming fully prepared to "die well"—whenever that may be.

●　　●　　●

"Finally, beloved, whatever is true, whatever is honorable, whatever is just, whatever is pure, whatever is pleasing, whatever is commendable, if there is any excellence and if there is anything worthy of praise, think about these things. Keep on doing the things that you have learned and received and heard and seen . . . and the God of peace will be with you" (Philippians 4:8-9).

POSTSCRIPT

Before Columbus set sail to cross the Atlantic, people believed that the world ended somewhere past Gibraltar. The royal motto said plainly, *"Ne Plus Ultra,"* meaning, "There is no more beyond here."

But when Columbus returned, he had actually discovered a whole new world. The ancient motto was now meaningless. In this crisis, someone made a noble and thrifty suggestion, which Queen Isabella acted upon. It was simply that the first word, *ne*, be deleted, leaving just two words: *"Plus ultra."*— "There is plenty more beyond here."

Plus ultra. There is plenty more beyond the point where you now find yourself. You may have been told that your illness *could* lead to your death, or your doctor's prognosis may have been much more specific. You have choices to make, and only you can make them. The only certainties you have are what you know from previous experience—and previous experience does not shed much light on your present circumstances.

I have written this book in the hope that it will help you to know that there is plenty more ahead of you. May the time remaining to you be filled with purpose and with enough energy to help you find ways to make your final days, weeks, months, or years meaningful, challenging, and fulfilling.

I commend you to the care and guidance of God through his Son, Jesus Christ. May God walk with you as you seek after and find the "plenty more" that lies beyond.

Know that my prayers are with you!